# MORE
# OR
# LESS

**Bill Knight**

# More or Less

**Set in 16pt Times New Roman**



---

Library of Congress Cataloging-In-Publication Data

Knight, Bill
More or Less / Bill Knight
p. (large print)
ISBN 1-4116-7942-3
1. Large type Books.
I. Title> Business & Economics
II. Series>Finance

For the love of my life, Donna;
My wife, my soul mate,
And the wind beneath my wings

## Prologue

The days of our lives are short! How we spend them and the decisions we make with our money and time determine the quality of life we will have as we age.

All the decisions in life are ours to make. We make them one at a time every single day we live.

Learning how to prepare for a secure financial future requires thought, study, and action.

The greatest destroyers of personal wealth building are debt and procrastination.

Only one of every hundred men and women alive today will live out their last days in comfort, dignity and independence.

This book is intended to be a presentation of simple truths that will assist you in making decisions that will bring you more money, more joy, more happiness, and more peace of mind.

Money will not buy any of us happiness but it will certainly be necessary to buy us almost everything else we need both now and throughout our lifetimes.

**More or Less---that is the choice**. You get to choose and you do so every time you take a dollar from your wallet or purse. Those simple day to day decisions determine the quality of your later life and while they may seem small and insignificant when considered as single events, in the grand scheme of things, they are critically important to your long-term quality of life and care.

What we all need is enough and then some. We need enough money and then some, enough time, enough health, enough love, happiness and personal peace.

Preparing properly for a dignified end of life without being a burden to anyone is a noble and worthwhile goal.

Fully enjoying the experience of living until its certain end is worthy of contemplation. Figuring out how to fund life is no small task and to do it well brings personal satisfaction and a feeling of "well done."

## The first thing you have to do

The first thing you have to do to accumulate wealth is to have a wealth-building mindset. Spenders never develop that mind-set and therefore they spend their lives earning money, taking on and then paying off debt, and wondering at the end of each day, week, and year where their money has gone. They receive their gratifications from the "feel goods" that come from quick thrills of feeling good about buying "stuff."

Others spend because they really believe they will never have anything anyway so why not enjoy the moment?

There is one truth that comes from a lifetime of watching people both earn and spend their money. Most never save! They never learn to save and never develop a wealth-building mindset.

So, whether you have ever had such a mindset or not, all you have to do is ***save a part of every dollar you ever earn!***

This book is not about quoting numbers so I will not. It is about giving you simple truths that will enable you to build wealth. As a practical application of this first key point, you must decide that you deserve wealth and that you will need money throughout your lifetime but especially near the end of your life. You must then realize that nobody else is going to do it for you and that the pressures for you to spend are enormous. You must toughen your mind set and commit to change.

**So, rule one for building wealth is committing to save part of every before tax dollar, every payday for the rest of your working life.**

## The second thing you have to do

The second thing you have to do is find out exactly where you are right now financially and compare the money coming in to the money going out. There can never be any accumulation of wealth or any peace of financial mind until the balance of financial power swings from others to you. In order to gain the financial advantage you must take your new wealth building mindset and realize fully that it will never be enough just to balance the money coming in to the money going out. It is a financial imperative that the "outflows" must always be less than the "inflows." To do otherwise is to mortgage your financial future.

**The simple stated rule is that you must spend less than you earn and you must have enough cash inflow to first fund your savings and then to pay your bills.**

## The third thing you have to do

When you consider all you own and then take away from that all you owe you come up with net worth. If you cashed everything out and paid off all your debts, what you are left with is what you have that will pay you income for the rest of your life.

This is a difficult process for most people because the things they own are "depreciating assets---'clothes, cars, furniture, etc'." Our goal is to accumulate "appreciating assets---'savings and investments'." We want to own things that will be worth more tomorrow than they are worth today.

Having been involved in both "living estate" sales (pre-death) and "estate" sales (post-death), rest assured that most of your worldly goods are worth about a dime on the dollar--- if that.

True wealth is the accumulation of things of monetary value that grow over time and pay you either dividends and/or income regularly. It is this latter type of wealth that will feed you and pay your medical bills in later life.

**The rule is to first calculate your present net worth and then to commit to grow it 15% per year every year of your life.**

## People plan and God laughs

Proper planning prevents poverty, bankruptcy, and lives of quiet desperation. We are in control of our financial destinies. Learning how to save, invest, and spend wisely are certainly things that are within our personal control.

In essence, the process boils down to some simple questions that need to be asked and answered.

The first question is, "Why do you want money? What does it mean to you?"

The next question is, "How much money does the things you want cost?" List them all and be as specific as possible. You can have anything you want but not everything.

The next question is, "How much money do you have?" Being able to know this is important. Whether it is a little or a lot is not the important thing. Knowing the number in total gives you your starting point.

The next question is, "What is the gap between the cost of what you want and what you have?" Knowing this allows you to properly prepare to fund your financial future.

The last question is, "Where is the plan to fill the gap?" **Without a plan---written down and committed to, you are unlikely to ever properly fund your dreams and desires.**

It is worthwhile for you, the reader, to stop right here and ponder both the simplicity and importance of these five questions.

As a professional strategic and operational planner for over 30 years prior to my retirement in 1997, I know that planning the future is both possible and necessary in order to chart a definite course of actions that take me in the direction of my goals.

All the while, even with best efforts, life seems to intervene regularly into our best-laid plans. Ill-timed events can and do cause havoc to our minds and wallets.

Taking charge of one's earthly life is within our control. So is living within our means, saving, and investing wisely.

## The art of counting money

When a dollar is taken from a wallet or purse, most people think it is just a dollar. Not to me! Never has been and never will be again.

A dollar is a precious commodity! Thinking of its future value and its purchasing power are the important considerations.

When a dollar is spent, it is gone! Unless you bought something that goes up in value or pays you interest or a dividend, you just "consumed" it. That is where the term consumer came from. Every merchant wants you to spend that dollar and so does the government. So, merchants and government are not your financial friends. They act like friends and make you think they have your best interests at heart. In truth, they do not.

If the dollar is left in a drawer for a year and then spent, it will not buy what a dollar would buy a year ago. Inflation ate part of it up and it is now worth less.

If the dollar is used to buy anything that depreciates in value it is no longer worth a dollar. You won't even be able to easily calculate what it is worth.

If the dollar is saved today and earns 4.5% for the next 30 years, it is not worth a dollar, it is worth $3.86. Every time you spend a single dollar, it is the same as taking $3.86 away from your financial future. Just to add insult to injury, that $3.86 you just spent on a coke would have paid you $.02 cents per month for 20 years after you retired. So, if you are thirty years away from retirement and can easily grab your wallet and whip out a dollar for some consumable item and feel good about it, you just do not have much of a grasp on how expensive your financial future is likely to be.

The power of a dollar is awesome. Either, "poof" it is gone or "wow" this dollar can really go to work for me. Fewer poofs and more wow is where we are going.

## Your greatest asset

Earning power is your greatest asset! That power is usually, but certainly not always, obtained through education. In theory, you get a good education, then get a good job, then make a lot of money, spend money and come out the other end of the tunnel well off and financially secure.

After fifteen years of working with the debt burdened, debt free, high earners, low earners, and everything in between, my experience has been that the amount of money you make has little to do with how much money you will either save or invest.

As an adjunct college professor, I met hundreds of students who were so consumed with credit card and student loan debt that they had already burdened their future earnings so severely that even with a great paying job it would be years, and in some cases decades, before they were un-burdened financially. That is not what we are trying to accomplish.

Go back to the first three rules. Save a part of every dollar, spend less than you earn and grow your net worth never change. Whether you are going to school or not you have to get and stay out of debt and grow your net worth. It can be done!

At a graduation ceremony, I spoke with a student who took great pride in having worked three jobs while in college, having no student loans, graduating with honors, and getting a high paying job right out of school. Now, that <u>is</u> what we want.

So, earning power plus an understanding of the three rules will give you a reasonable chance for financial success. Anything less is a "trip up fool's hill" as my Mother (God rest her soul) used to say.

Education, both formal and informal, is a critical ingredient to the "money cake" we are baking. Lifetime learning is an imperative! The more you know, you more you can earn from others who are willing to pay to know what you know or to at least pay you a decent wage to do what you do for them so they can make a profit for themselves from your labors.

## Financial independence

Imagine what for you would be a perfect day. From the moment you wake up until the moment you go to sleep. What did you do specifically? If time was your own and you had enough money to do whatever you chose to do all day long, how would that feel?

Financial independence is that moment when your money earns enough money to pay all your bills and leaves you with some left over to cover emergencies. It is that quiet still moment when it dawns on you that time is your own. You can be anywhere you choose to be doing whatever it is you choose to do and you can afford to be there.

Tomorrow's financial independence is a planned event. By doing more of the right things every day, you will enhance your chances of reaching financial independence sooner.

The vast majority of people with whom I have come into contact and worked with over these last fifteen years have absolutely no clue as to how much money they will need to enjoy a comfortable older age. They have never calculated, nor had anyone else calculate, what they will most likely need in order to live and die with dignity and independence. They have no plans, no calculations, and have had no conversations of substance on this subject with anyone. So, they just live day to day hoping it will all work out.

Money saved and invested wisely over the working life of any individual or family can be sufficient to fund a financially independent lifestyle. It cannot be achieved by anyone who does not spend less than they earn, save some of every dollar, learn how to invest conservatively and wisely, and grow their net worth steadily.

So, there you have it. Financial independence is a choice. You make that choice every single day with every single dollar that comes into your possession. You either are marching in the direction of your goals and dreams or you are stuck where you are.

## Dollars per day of life

One action that works to help focus your mind on the task ahead is to perform a simple calculation. All you need do is add up how many days you have lived on this earth and then divide that number into the total amount of money you have available to you now from your checking, savings, and investment accounts only. To retire comfortably you will need that number to be at least $50 and preferably $75 per day of life.

Why don't you calculate your number right now and see how well you are doing?

The hard part is getting together that first $10,000. Think about it! For the first eighteen years of life you earn virtually nothing and are taken care of by parents or loved ones. Then, you get a job or go off to college and earn very little for the first few years after that. If all goes well you get a decent job, pay your taxes, choose your lifestyle, and begin to accumulate stuff.

The difference lies right there! What kind of stuff will you accumulate? If you acquire debt, you must attach to that debt the absolute, mandatory mindset to get rid of it as fast as you can. Preferably, except for big ticket items like cars and houses, you want to avoid debt. It is the great destroyer of wealth!

Even to do it right is a challenge because buying cars, houses, getting married, having babies, and buying stuff is a part of being young. You will do some or maybe all of these things and you will be funding them at a time when you have probably the least amount of earning power you will ever have. It is no wonder young people go astray and pile up debt and mortgage their futures. Advertisers make it seem so easy and it is easy! That's the problem---you fall for it. Why should you destroy your financial future just because you were enticed into bad financial behaviors?

Oh! By the way, you should also calculate your days of life against your total net worth figure. Independent living will require a resulting number approaching $150 per day of life.

## Life energy

Wasting a moment of your life doing anything you do not now and never did really want to do is a waste of your most precious commodity---your life energy.

Why people spend their time doing work that does not interest or challenge them just to make another dollar so they can pay their bills so they can do it all over again tomorrow and the day after that makes me sad.

By working with those nearing the ends of their lives, never once has any one of them every said they wished they had worked harder and made another dollar.

Having worked for many years now with those of age, experience, and infirmity, how common we all really are as we near the end of our lives has been my biggest surprise.

In those final months, weeks, and days of life there are but three things that remain common to all with whom my volunteer work has been done. The first is always, “forgive me”, the second is “I love you”, and the third is always “goodbye.” Never once have I ever heard anything about work or money---never once.

So, there must be a life lesson buried in here somewhere. I think it may be to live every day as if it were your last---it well might be.

Choose those with whom you want to live your life carefully. Accentuate the positives! Find work that interests you and that challenges your inner self.

Understand the precious nature of life and be prayerful and grateful for the health, happiness, and personal peace that life offers.

Pause to ponder those who are now in the way of your happiness. Those who have troubled souls offer you very little. You can support them and love them but you do not have to be around them or interact with them.

Life energy is a precious commodity. The last thing you want to ever have to do is remember a life full of regrets.

## My hospice training and what I learned

After weeks of training, in our final meeting with the hospice staff, my greatest personal lesson about this important work was learned.

Imagine the room with me and go there with me. There are ten terrified direct-care volunteers surrounded by hospice trainers and the hospice chaplain. It has just hit us square between the eyes that the easy part is over. All the training has been given and now we are about to graduate and be assigned our first patients. The room was still and quiet and there was a reverence there that never before in my life and never since have I ever experienced.

Frightening me is not an easy thing to do but at that moment, my nerves were really on edge.

Then, sensing something was wrong with the crowd, the chaplain asked for a show of hands of anyone in the room who was apprehensive about what they were about to do. Ten hands shot straight up seemingly all at once. I know there was only a second's pause before mine went up.

He was the only one who laughed out loud! His next words will follow me all the remaining days of my life and to him and for those words I remain eternally grateful.

He said and I quote him now, "This work is so important; it is ok to do it badly for you are among the few who do it at all."

From that moment to this, never once has my ability to work with people at or near the end of their lives ever bothered me.

My first patient, we will call him M, had a fantastic sense of humor. He was married to the love of his life and their love for each other was apparent. My most beautiful memory of M was when he asked me to call his brother for him. I knew he did not have a brother but I dialed at random anyway and handed him the phone. He had a great chat with his brother and then gave me back the phone. That call brought him peace and he smiled. On another occasion, my wife, Donna (a direct care volunteer also) took M's wife out to get her hair done and do some shopping. When they returned, M heard them coming in and said loudly, "Get the dancing girls out of here, the wives are home!" On my last visit before he died, he was in enormous pain from pancreatic cancer and the high dose morphine patch was not enough to keep him pain free. A quick call and the hospice nurse came running and doubled the dosage on the patch and he relaxed and rested. There were times when I just got to talk to M and pray with him and sometimes we sang a song or two---badly, I might add.

What struck me about him was the grace and dignity with which he and his wife handled this situation. She had a cancer growing on the side of her face but would not have it cared for until he was gone.

Their modest financial affairs were all in order and she lives today in their home, cancer free.

It is from M that I got affirmations about living. He had lived modestly but enjoyed what he had earned. He had an obvious love for his wife and it showed.

They had taken the time, long before the need appeared, to plan for disease, infirmity, and death.

Never once did he complain. Never once did he do anything but live fully.

My only regret is that I never knew him before his illness; he was one heck of a nice man.

So, my takeaways from M are, you never have to be in pain as you near the end of your life and you can be kept comfortable. Its formal name is palliative care. To me it means anyone can be kept comfortable and pain free no matter how diseased their physical body may be. Also, he taught me to keep laughing and loving and being proud of what you have accomplished with your life.

The story of M is but the first of several that hopefully add some insights to you, the reader.

One thing always interesting to me is asking the questions, "How would I act if it were my turn to die. Are all my affairs in order if that time were to come today?"

## The financially foolish

Students on a university campus can sure demonstrate some foolish financial behaviors to their adjunct professors---especially to me. Imagine just coming from the home of a hospice patient and arriving on campus to grab a bite of lunch at the cafeteria.

As I walk out of the lunch room with my food, I see two tables set up just to the left. Both are credit card company representatives offering $3,000 credit cards to any and everyone who comes by.

The line is long and the representatives use short forms to expedite the process. Never once do they explain the financial consequences of their benevolence.

Then, over the next three years of teaching, the foolish stories of debt already accumulated surround me.

Would you believe? No money to buy the textbook but over $24,000 worth of credit card debt before age twenty paying an average of 18.9% interest. As if that is not bad enough another $21,000 worth of outstanding student loans.

How about this? A coke a candy bar and some chips before my night class. Poof, life-time money consumed without thought in an instant.

My personal favorite is this one. “I’m never going to have anything anyway, so I spend what I have now---what’s wrong with that?”

The list goes on and on. They just don’t get it and never will so long as they continue to ignore the obvious need they will have for money later in life.

This is not some silly game that can be played as if it did not matter. Life is hard and getting the advantage with money onto your side requires planning, discipline, and commitment.

Frittering away precious dollars and paying interest to others so they can get wealthy off of you makes no sense at all to me.

Once individuals learn bad financial habits, they follow them all the days of their lives.

## The consequences of instant financial gratification

Over and over, day after day, my travels have brought me into contact with people who simply cannot and will not delay their gratifications. They want it all and they want it all right now.

One such story is one of my former students, D. He was a fine student, conscientious and talented. He did well in my Entrepreneurship class and during it we were able to build for him a debt elimination plan that was customized to his specific circumstances. A year later, he graduated. The first thing he did was he got married and for each of the next three years, each fall, he and his wife had a baby. He had an interest only mortgage on a home he got from a builder at an inflated price. He was in debt for not only his home but also for his two nearly new cars, and for all the consumer debt his three credit cards would allow. By the way, he was working at a commission only job where he was the junior member of the staff during this entire period. His wife was at home with two toddlers and an infant and they could not even afford a small payment per week so she could have a "mother's day out." He told me he had dutifully tried to pay off his debts before he got out of college using the debt elimination plan we created. He told me he just could not bring himself to deprive himself of all the things he saw others buy and have. He just wanted it all and he wanted it all right now. Just recently I learned that he lost his job. Can you imagine what he, his wife, and his family will now endure as they try to rebuild their lives----not their financial lives----their lives.

All this was avoidable for them just as it is avoidable for you. Making the conscious decisions to delay your gratifications and to gradually build the "things" of life (where there is little value anyway) is a far richer and much more satisfying way to live.

D stays in contact with me and we have offered on numerous occasions to help him and his family. He has always and continues to refuse our help. He wants to do it on his own. I bet he will now.

## Grab last year's income tax return

First, let me ask you this question. "Does the federal government take its share of every dollar you ever earn, every dollar of interest you ever earn, every dividend dollar you ever earn, and a little less than half of what's left when you die if you haven't planned your estate carefully?"

Of course they do! They do so because they know how to pay themselves first. Just the lesson I want you to adopt for yourself!

One of the easiest teaching tools I've been able to find simply asks you to drag out your last filed tax return. Look at the total amount of income you made and ask yourself this question, "How much of that total sum of money do I still have?" If you don't have any of it left or if you have very little of it left, you are not on your way to financial health and independence.

For so long as I can remember, it has been my firm belief that the first time every American was paid their total wage in cash and then they had to go window to window handing out cash for each separate tax deduction that comes from their paycheck before they ever see it, it would be the last time Americans would tolerate such a system of deductions. Our government understands how money works. They pay themselves first and last. You get the crumbs in the middle.

Wealth accumulation is not about how much money flows into your life, it is about how much money is left after you earn what you earn and spend what you spend. It is the money that sticks and stays with you that you will use to save, invest and properly prepare for your costly financial future.

So, if at the end of the day, week, year and/or decade, you have nothing to show for your work, how on earth do you think you will fund your later years?

By not saving and not investing you have made the decision to be taken care of, without dignity, by the very government that took the lion's share of your money from you in the first place.

## From wealth and comfort to financial peril

About two years ago, I met with a wonderful couple we will call J and his wife R. For all of their married life they had enjoyed the fruits of their labors. They had enough money for not only a wonderful home in a wonderful neighborhood but also great schools for the kids and many luxuries of life. They saved dutifully too and their wealth was accumulating nicely.

Then, the unthinkable happened. J lost his job! He thought he would find another one quickly. He did not! The savings began to dwindle and he decided to invest in a business. His stake in that business is now worthless. R opened a small business out of necessity. It does not make much money but she loves it. It does help pay the bills and it remains open today.

When I met them at my office, they had just enough cash to buy gas to get home. My advice was harsh! Sell the big house and hoard cash and squarely face the financial situation they now found themselves experiencing. Tears flowed from all of us. It was a horrible afternoon for them and for me too because, in this case, these bad events really did happen to people who were doing a lot of things right.

The reason for telling this story is because they still live in that big house in that nice neighborhood. He still has not found a permanent job that pays anywhere near what his old one paid and they simply have not and will not accept the fact that their previous financial lives are gone. Their savings are now almost totally gone.

Getting them and many others to face squarely "head on" the financial challenges they face has been one of my biggest frustrations as a professional financial planner.

You cannot and must not live in the past or dwell on what once was. Only by starting over and doing things right again will they ever have any chance of achieving financial independence.

## Why you must do it yourself

In the course of my work with wealthy people who pay me an annual retainer to serve as their financial advisor and executive assistant, I meet with stock brokers and brokerages that have held themselves out as fiduciaries of my client's brokerage accounts.

Here are but a few of my horror stories. Three year's ago, we went to see a broker who I believed was buying things for the client without authorization, buying inappropriate things for him, and failing to return his phone calls. When we went to see the broker in his office and laid out the case that he had lost the client over $250,000 because of his inappropriate buys and sells, the broker responded this way. "Yes! I did do all those things. I am on the school board now and I don't have much time to review client accounts and I've just been doing what I can when I can." He never denied one single thing. At least he was honest about that. We removed all remaining funds from that brokerage and broker and my client never received back one penny of his lost money.

Another case involved a friend who thought his wife's broker had sold her an inappropriate annuity. He asked me to join the conversation at his home with the broker present. I did! When I asked him about what fees she was being charged and what return she was getting, he went berserk—started screaming and yelling. We caught him red handed making money for himself at the client's expense.

Another case involved a CPA who had his clients, now mine, in inappropriately risky investments. He had not found out what their risk tolerances were and he had been losing money for them for years before they fired him and hired me.

Stockbrokers pride themselves on beating the market. If the market is down 20%, they want to be praised when they only lose you 15%. Such logic will make you quite poor if you fall for it.

Your money must always go up in value---never down!

My purpose in telling but a few of the dozens of bad experiences I have personally witnessed and been a part of is not to condemn the entire industry but to identify for you that nobody cares as much about your money as you do. Some in fact, care far more about finding some way to get you to pay them an annual percentage of your total wealth year after year, whether they have made you any money or not, than they do about caring for your money once they become its custodian.

My stories come from actual events in some of America's largest brokerage firms. They are real and they really happened and my clients lost large portions of their wealth. Losses that were preventable! That is the point. Preventable!

Until you have built dollar sums large enough to produce sufficient income to pay all your bills and then some, you have no business risking one penny of your hard earned money.

Learning how to save and find the best interest rates available so that your savings will grow steadily should be one of your top priorities.

For the last five years, the vast majority of money being managed by others for the investor has underperformed the yields that come from simply saving your money and finding the highest yields available to magnify each dollar's power.

Stock picking is for professionals and not very many of them are any good at it. The average man or woman in America is far better off today learning how to build their wealth slowly, steadily, and reliably.

I recently came back from a meeting where my financial planning associate's conversations at both lunch and dinner centered on what their present fees were and how much more they thought they could get by creating new offerings. To my dismay, their focus was on "their wealth"---not on their client's.

Since only one of every hundred people alive today will retire with full dignity and financial independence, it is my pleasure to tell you that you can be that one. Being perceived as odd or financially different is a badge worn by me with honor.

## The leaks in your money boat

Creating and implementing financial plans for people has been a part of my life for the last fifteen years. Some have a lot of money, some have very little money, and some are in debt up to their ears.

The process we follow is always the same. We identify what comes in and then identify what goes out. When the "ins" is bigger than the "outs," we build a strategy for growing wealth conservatively over time. When the "outs" are bigger than the "ins," we develop a plan to either get more coming in or less going out.

What I want to emphasize here is that never in fifteen years of building plans for individuals have I ever failed to find at least 20% cash outflow leakage. Yes! The average is 20%!

The objective eye of an interested third party will most likely find that same or even greater leakage in your cash outflows.

One client had a cost of $1,200 a year for carpet cleaning. She had an accident prone dog. We put vinyl tile in her kitchen for $400 and now the accidents still occur with the same frequency but they cost 66% less.

That same client spent $480 per month at her golf club. The same club she had not visited in over eight months.

Another client paid $1,200 a year to a tennis club for the family. Not one family member had been inside the club for over two years.

Most clients do not shop their "big ticket" items like home, car, and life insurances annually when the renewal notices arrive. This is a costly mistake. Many times, for many varying reasons, rates change for the better. If you do not shop those rates and just write the check when the annual invoices arrive, you are simply giving away money----leaking like a sieve to use my terms.

The key point here is to stimulate you to analyze every single bill you pay. Stopping leakage is important financial work.

## Life planning

One of the most powerful forces available to individuals is the creation of a life plan. Creating the format is the easy part. Filling in the blanks will force you to face your personal thoughts and, done properly, will serve as an important guide as you age.

There are five headings. Across the top of a page of paper, left to right, write personal, professional, educational, financial, and fun.

Then, down the left side of the page write the decades of your life starting with 20's, then 30's, then 40's---up to the 90's.

Now, look on the chart and fill in the blanks. The 20's should be easy if you are in your 30's. You have already lived that decade. You may find you have nothing in one box and six things in another. There is no right or wrong!

One great story, and my favorite, is a client who hired me to do a life plan for him. After three submissions to me of his best thinking, I had to tell him his work was pitiful. It was obvious that he was living a one dimensioned life and his accomplishments as a professional were being completed at the expense of each of the other four categories. He was challenged to try again and to stretch himself to realize what he really wanted to do with his life.

By the way, he was a general manager of a Fortune 50 company at the time this work was being done and he was making "big bucks."

His next submission was fully filled out and it was obvious to me that he had experienced a personal epiphany.

After discussions and confirmations, he left his job in big business and became a priest. I know he is happy because he told me he was.

As this story illustrates, this tool will change your life if you will let it.

Everybody needs to spend some time thinking about their lives and how they want to live them as they age.

This tool has been a part of my life for over forty years.

## Who has the monetary advantage?

The vast majority of people never consider who has the monetary advantage in a financial transaction. To me, it is absolutely essential that I both get and keep that advantage at all times. To do this, you must consider first what it is.

Monetary advantage goes to the person or firm that makes or saves money from the transaction.

So, when you order new checks from the bank, if you pay for them, they have the advantage. If you get them and their use for free, then you have the advantage. Paying someone to give me the right to access my own money violates my soul.

Paying account services fees is another example. When you pay them, they have the advantage. Refusing to pay them and having them removed is your duty. Again, it is your money.

If an item you want costs $20 and you offer $10 and buy it for $15, you just got a $5 advantage you would not have gotten had you not asked. Never be too embarrassed to offer less. All they can say is no and then you can walk away and that is your final say.

Refusing to be persuaded that a high price is a good price is something that takes a strong will to deal with. Everything is on sale somewhere all the time. Your job is to find the exact same item at a lower price.

Value is built into a home not when you sell it but when you buy it. Buying at a value price is key to the future success you will have selling it for a profit.

Over time, you will instinctively react negatively to anyone and/or anything that attempts to deprive you of the financial advantage. You will know that the dollar saved is far more valuable to your future than is the dollar squandered.

One primary difference between the financially secure and those who struggle financially is which side of the check they sign. The wealthy sign the back (depositing money) while those who struggle continue to sign the front (spending money).

## Inexpensive traditions as wealth building tools

One of the richest experiences of our married life is my and Donna's Valentine's tradition. Long ago, when we had absolutely nothing but children and debts, we found a fun way to express our love for each other that continues today.

First, we go to a card store. She carefully and privately chooses three cards while I do the same. Then, we give them to each other. We usually laugh out loud and then give each other a big hug and kiss and put them back on the shelf.

From there we go to the grocery store. I always reach in the refrigerated case and select for her a beautiful arrangement. I get it out and give it to her. We laugh and hug again. Then, we put the flowers back in the case and walk away.

With that done, she always gets to hold a stuffed animal and she also gets to hold candy. I choose each very carefully for she is indeed a very special love.

We put everything we have touched back where we got it and then leave giggling and holding hands.

I used to add up my savings but gave that up once I knew I could afford to do it all if I had to. Conservatively, our Valentine's routine saves us at least $100 in today's money which is worth far more than that over our remaining lifetime.

That is just our Valentine's tradition. We have similar traditions for Christmas and birthdays but I'll leave those to your imaginations. You can rest assured that they do not cost money.

Our forty-three year marriage is based on genuine love and friendship.

Our comfortable retirement came from mutual hard-work, patience, planning, dreaming, and understanding.

We are both 62 today and we have been comfortably retired for almost a decade.

We are by no means cheap. We live well and travel extensively and take pride in our financial and personal accomplishments. We just had different goals!

## The theory of 300 sweaters

Most people think they need 300 sweaters. Each day they try to accumulate another, then another, and then another. After a while they have at least 300 sweaters.

They work each day at a job that may or may not satisfy their inner selves and they do it because they want another sweater.

They leave their loved ones and sometimes are gone for long periods in search of another sweater.

They seldom have time to wear even one sweater but they always are in search of another one.

Never are they satisfied with what they have and they remain blinded to all but the quest for the acquisition of another sweater. For years and years they just accumulate sweaters.

Then, when 300 sweaters would obviously be enough for almost anyone, they just continue acquiring them. They continue to toil doing things they don't like because it is what they do and they walk around wondering why they are not happy.

Far more satisfying would be the duty to give away some of those sweaters to those who would need, appreciate and use them; keeping just enough of them to meet your needs and keep you warm.

My hope is that it is obvious to you that this story is not about sweaters at all. It is about the quest for money.

Accumulating money just for the sake of accumulating it will not satisfy the needs of your soul.

The quest is for enough money to live comfortably and debt free. Your need is for enough to not have to sell your soul to an employer doing a job that does not now or never has satisfied your inner needs.

Throughout my lifetime, time after time, my observations and conversations have led me to the conclusion that most people are indeed living lives of quiet desperation seeing no way out of their current circumstances and shackled to jobs and lives that bring them little personal peace and happiness.

## Bum—homeless or outdoorsman

During my lifetime, one of my choices has been to study "perceptions."

During this last fifteen years as a professional financial planner, my perceptions have been altered somewhat when it comes to understanding how people think about their money and money management.

If I tell you a man is a bum, would you think it is his fault?

If I tell you that man is not a bum, he is just homeless. Would you think it is society's fault?

If I tell you he is neither a bum nor homeless but that he is instead an outdoorsman would you conclude that he had made a personal choice?

What you need to know is that each of these three is the exact same person.

It is the perception that we place on each word that makes the difference in whether we believe it is their fault, society's fault, or their personal choice.

From experience, our society for some reason that makes no sense to me, perceives that those who have the most money must be the financial outdoors people. They must have chosen to be that way or been lucky enough to get that way while the rest of us did less well, either through a fault of our own or because of circumstances beyond our control.

The financially homeless are perceived to have made bad choices. They must have squandered their chance because of some restriction placed on them by someone else. That is the perception.

Financial bums are perceived as those who have no money, no access to money, and little chance of ever having any money. The perception is that it is their fault.

My perception, and the financial reality, is that all those who make a conscious choice to save and invest a portion of every dollar they ever earn will be neither a bum nor homeless—ever.

## Blinded by your employer's light

Have you ever been so close to something that you could not see it?

Your employer, the source of your income, consumes your day, and mentally consumes much more of your mental energy than that.

They train you to think their way and to identify with their culture and customs. You must conform if you are to be a part of what they are doing.

In their quest to achieve their goals, either intentionally or un-intentionally, they rob (yes---rob, steal, take from you) some very precious things. They take you many times away from those you love either in late or early morning hours or in travel for days and sometimes weeks and months at a time.

All this time devoted to a job steals the days and hours that should be used in pursuing your dreams, loves and passions.

There are many things to do with one's life and the job you now hold is just one of them. There are millions of others.

Have you ever felt "trapped" at work? Have you ever wished you were home for the love of family and friends instead of sitting with a group of business associates in some hotel and/or restaurant playing like you were having a good time? I have--- plenty of times.

The moral of this story is to be realistic about who you are and the price you pay to carry your current title and earn your current living.

Live in the moment! Savor the love of your soul mate and your children. Squandering one moment is a moment lost forever.

Doing anything for or with anyone that is not what you want to do cheapen your personal worth.

If I had it to do all over again, I would have been home much more doing the things I like to do with the people I like to do them with.

## Enough or too little or too much

Several years ago, just outside Banff, Canada at Lake Louise, Donna and I were just sitting on the hillside watching the beauty of the Canadian Rockies. My mind started to wander.

I wondered first if there would be enough money for us to live the rest of our lives in comfort. Then, I wondered, "What if it wasn't enough?" That led me to the next question, "What if it was too much?"

As the afternoon flew by in such a naturally beautiful setting, it came time for me to face some realities.

What we have is ours and it is hard earned. Whether it is enough or not is not for me to know.

My life is filled with the richness of experiences that can never be either changed or traded.

There are transitions in life and mine had just occurred (retired from my professional life).

My "for pay" period was over. While working for money has occurred from time to time since then when people or projects have interested me, it will never again be a dominant driver in my life.

My quest is for more time to be with those who share my name and who love me for who and what I am or ever will be.

It was time to find an inner-peace which is now all mine. During my working years that peace eluded me although I tried hard to find it and had come close to finding it several times. It is indeed a peace that passes understanding.

What those questions taught me that day and each day since is the importance of living in the moment. The importance of never settling for less than what it is that you really want out of life.

My work with senior citizens and hospice patients and their families has taught me how incredibly short life really is and when one works with our seniors regularly it does not take long to realize that they too know how precious every breath taken truly is.

Maybe you should schedule a trip to Lake Louise.

## Four priorities you should use

Often, the hardest thing to figure out is how to get started doing something that you know is important to your future.

Every man, woman, and family should take the time to execute the following four financial activities.

You have to first set financial goals. What is it you are trying to do or get done? Do you want to retire early, buy and pay cash for a first home, send the children to the finest schools, travel extensively? Figuring out what it is you want to do and when you want to do it is half the battle. The other half is finding a way to fund the activities at the times you need them to be funded.

After goal setting, it is time to lay out a detailed written plan for getting there. Part of the planning includes determining how much you can reasonably expect to earn from the job you now hold and the investments you now have and the ones you will make during the remainder of your lifetime. Above all else, commit the plan to paper. **No goal has any power until it is written down.**

Then, you have to determine your time horizons. Figuring out how much money you will have one year from today, three years from now, a decade from now, and thirty years or more out is important work and it should be undertaken seriously and updated regularly. The goal is for it to be "roughly right."

Lastly, you must decide what risks you can tolerate and still sleep at night. Knowing this up front helps you weather the inevitable financial and market storms that will come up during your lifespan.

For most people, zero risk is the best planning assumption. If you know nothing about the stock market and have no inclination to learn, you are far better off to diligently save your money, lose not a single dollar ever, and earn the highest interest rates available every day of your life.

So, there you have it. Set goals, formalize the plan, determine your time horizons, decide your risk tolerances and implement. Then, update the plan often and monitor the growth day after day.

## The best laid plans

Let me tell you about D and his wife E. D was a planner. He was a good steward of his money and he owned seven small life insurance policies he had bought over the years to make sure E would be comfortable when he died. All his financial records were in order and well kept by E (unusual in my experience that a wife actually took care of the family money). She was detail oriented and comfortable discussing money matters (another unusual finding---two taboo subjects to most people are discussing their money and discussing death).

D and E moved into a duplex on the campus of a senior home and lived for a short time independently. Then, suddenly, D's health failed. The disease he had was horrible. It paralyzed his body gradually and his speech too. Now, E had the burden of paying for the duplex on campus and for nursing home care too.

D lived far longer than he would have wanted. Every day, E dressed him and stayed with him as his body turned to stone.

As you might expect, D died months later and by then we had been able to make sure all the financial paperwork of both their lives was in order. Each of us thought, and D, before his death, knew that E would be comfortable in her old age because he had done a good job of accumulating insurances.

Then, the story gets ugly. It took us over a year to collect the proceeds from the insurance policies. Not because we did not try and not because we did not repeatedly ask for the money and prove that it was due E by providing death certificates and letters requesting payment.

Each of the seven insurance companies drug its feet. Writing letters making offers of options E could choose that would keep the money with them and not send the money to her. It was disgusting.

Finally, we got her the insurance proceeds. In the meantime, she had to move into an off campus apartment, conserve her cash, and live a life that would have infuriated D had he been alive.

## My favorite earthly angel

In hospice work, special by its very nature, you come in contact with people who are so extraordinarily different that you have a hushed reverence in their presence.

Let me tell you about K. We met at a patient's home. I was there to assist the wife with financial matters and she was with the patient who was dying of aggressive facial cancer. He was a former military officer and a prideful and powerful man.

Through the doorway I could hear her conversation with him and her words to him were words of comfort and understanding. As she spoke them, she was removing the mask from his devastated face and cleansing his wounds and administering pain relieving morphine patches. I knew right then she was special.

We both happened to finish our work about the same time and we walked outside together.

Before I go any further, I should tell you that K wears big thick glasses because she does not see very well and hasn't for a very long time. I had noticed them but never thought a thing about them until that walk outside that home that day.

I told her I admired her ability to deal so effortlessly with such a horrific set of wounds and be so calm and thorough and gentle as she did her work.

To which, she replied, "Why do you think God made me almost blind? It was so that I could do this type of work." Her words to me that day overpowered my thoughts. Her affliction had become her gift---a gift she used to do good for others.

Now, all these years later, after many life experiences with K as we both did our hospice work, there is something so special about her that my determination and conviction is that she is different from the rest of us. She truly understands the meaning of life and is at peace with who she is and what she does. She was born to do this work and both she and everyone around her know it too. If the doctor told me today that I was dying, my first call would be to Donna and my second to K.

## The most important person in your life

Over the last several decades, my speaking and teaching engagements have all included what for me is a very special learning experience for the audiences.

The only question asked to individuals in front of the audience is, "Who is the most important person in your life and what did they teach you?"

When that question is asked quickly, I have seen grown men and women break into tears almost instantly. Some freeze in their tracks and do not want to answer at all because it is so personal. Still others never hesitate and smile as they almost instantly give their answer.

It is my honor to share the results with you from audiences who have answered this question from the coast of California to the coast of Florida and numerous cities and states in between.

Never once, not a single time has anyone ever mentioned a boss. Ninety nine percent of the time with thousands in the sample, the answer is always someone you love or someone that loves you or both. It is a father, a mother, a sister, a brother, an aunt or an uncle or a long gone relative. It is someone who nurtured you and taught you either at their bosom or at their knee. The outlying one percent occurred just a few years ago and it was a mentor. He was a man who had decided that he alone was going to commit his life to the betterment of another life. That is just what he did and the man he mentored recognized him as the most important person in his life.

So, there you have it. As much as we associate with workmates on the job, they may become our friends but they will never become the most important people in your life if my three decade sample is any indication.

By the way, the what they taught you is usually, how to trust, how to love and be loved, how to persevere, how to get up and go again, how to set goals, how to believe in yourself and how to stand on your own two feet and be proud.

## Insuring against poverty

It is indeed a rare person who does not have some form of insurance. You are insuring your car, your home, your health, disability, personal injury, fire, flood, and on and on and on. Each of these is what I called "perceived need" insurances.

You have no option but to buy insurance if you cannot make at least a 20% down payment on your home or if you have to finance the purchase of a car. The lender will not even give you the loan unless their risk is insured by you with you paying the full premium.

My concern for you is the "real" insurance you better have if you plan not to be eating from the dog food aisle at the discount supermarket where you will be shopping when you can no longer work and have to retire.

Let's say you want your savings and investments to pay you a modest $2,000 a month for 30 years. You know you can earn 4.5% safely and that your tax rate is 28%. Inflation is averaging 2.5% so you use that figure also. So, you earn 4.5%, take away what the tax man got (1.26% of the 4.5%) and take away also the 2.5% inflation. You are left with .74% (less than 1%) of the original 4.5% you earned.

Now, we have all we need to calculate the amount of money you must have invested to generate your desired level of income ($2,000) for thirty years. You need $645,502.16 in the bank working for you today.

If you want $5,000 a month, using the same inputs, you need $1,613,755.41.

The vast majority of people in this country today fully fund their "perceived need insurances," (all the things that rarely if ever will actually happen) and completely neglect the "real need" insurance they definitely will need to have as they enter their retirement years. The time to start saving is right now.

## Consumer debt elimination plan

Have you ever noticed how easy it is to get into debt and how hard it is to get out?

There is actually one simple reason why debt is so prevalent in our country.

Someone who has money has made it available to you. Since you cannot delay gratification, you are eager to take it from them even though they charge you an interest premium higher than they could get anywhere else and you take it, pay them their handsome interest rate for long periods of time, and thereby mortgage your future and enrich theirs.

Whipping out your wallet or purse and using one of your credit cards is no longer just convenience. It is habit! This habit of using the plastic cards has plunged our nation into its greatest personal debt total in recorded history.

For those of you who may have overdone the use of your cards just a smidge, here are suggestions on how you can set your jaw, grit your teeth, and dig your way out from under the debt pile you have already created.

List the names of each and every creditor, list the amounts you owe each creditor, list the interest rate you pay each creditor, list the minimum monthly amount you must pay each creditor, add up the number of creditors you owe, add up the total amount of money you owe, and average the interest rate you are paying to all your creditors.

Then, when the tears melt away, create a simple attack plan to eliminate all consumer debt in the shortest possible time.

To do this, pay off the highest interest rate debt first. Then, pay off the next highest and so on down the list. Each time you pay one off, add its payment to the next one and do it again and again until they are all gone.

Then, with them gone, breathe a sigh of relief and never allow the monetary advantage to slip away from you again—ever.

Debt is the great destroyer of wealth.

## A lesson taught to executives in Cincinnati

A fortune 50 company hired me to help their management team begin to think outside the box. They wanted me to give them new energy, passion, and zeal for the tough tasks that lay ahead of them.

When I arrived early at the auditorium where I would be speaking, I was alone. I taped a twenty dollar bill under a seat on the left, a fifty dollar bill under a seat on the right, and a hundred dollar bill under the seat directly in front of the podium where I would be standing to speak.

My motivational speech was a success and they rewarded it with a standing ovation. That made my next step easy. I thanked them and asked them to remain standing.

I told them that money and opportunity were all around them and they didn't even know it. I walked to the young woman who was standing in front of the seat where I had taped the twenty dollar bill. I asked her to turn over her chair. She did! She found the twenty and we all had a big laugh. I went on to explain to the standing audience that that wasn't so hard---was it?

The audience then did exactly what I thought they would do. As I walked back to the podium, every single person in the room but one sat down. One young man began to wander the room turning over empty chairs while everyone else stared at him wondering what he was doing. Nobody else got up.

By chance, the young man found the fifty dollar bill taped under an empty seat. He screamed and held it up. The room went nuts.

Needless to say, the audience tore that place apart. A near riot broke out. Chairs were being flipped over, people were running around flipping over empty chairs and when the hundred dollar bill was found a second level of chaos followed.

Needless to say, when I left that auditorium that day, the crowd had learned something and the janitorial staff had a lot of work to do to restore the auditorium.

## Pillars of financial independence

Of every hundred people alive today in the USA, 35 will not live to see age 65. Part of the reason why is the stress and strain that comes from trying to make ends meet in a world full of easy credit and instant gratification. It has been estimated that 90% of arguments around the home are related to money. Not about too much money, but about too little.

As for Social Security, just imagine trying to live on a monthly check that is two-thirds less than the monthly check you cannot live on now. Won't that be fun?

As for pensions, yours may or may not be there. Tens of thousands of defined benefit plans have been dropped and employers now offer savings vehicles that let you assume all the risks. If you lose it, it is gone forever. Not their fault and they owe you nothing else.

Americans during the 50's, 60's, and 70's saved 11% of their gross wages. By the 90's that number had melted to 4% and today, as I write this, the number is negative---less than nothing is being saved.

What this tells me is that a typical baby boomer (born between 1946-1964) who earns $50,000 and saves nothing will have to work until the day they die to maintain their current lifestyle.

With today's low interest rates, it will take $1,000,000 in investments just to earn $44,300 a year pre-tax.

This is not being written to frighten the elderly. Nothing is being said here that they do not already know.

Nor is it being written to startle the baby boomers. Reality will hit them soon enough.

It is being written for those of you who are still young enough to do something about it to make sure it does not happen to you.

You must save, save, save! Supersavers save 25% or more of gross income, solid savers save 10%, and most save nothing at all.

## Find a hobby that makes money

Many years ago, I took a course in wealth building that had a chapter in it that has served me well. It was a chapter about finding hobbies that created income not expenses.

It took me years to really figure out how to apply that lesson but it finally came to me.

Over the years, I have owned and operated a scholarship search business (while our children were in college), a financial newsletter, a financial planning business, a money school, a business advisory firm, and now two web sites, a consulting firm, and a book publication in addition to my jobs before retirement.

Each activity has produced income. It has created what I term "complimentary" money coming in. This is money that would not otherwise have been there.

Now, long retired, those streams of income not only produced income above and beyond what we were spending but it also has allowed us to travel extensively and do virtually whatever we want whenever we want. We saved it, did not spend it, and now it works for us every day producing new dollars we do not have to go out into the workplace to earn.

Think opportunistically! What are you good at and what could you sell that others would pay to know or have.

The last day you will ever work is the first day you fall in love with what you are doing. If your primary job does not offer you either sufficient monetary or psychic rewards, start something on your own using your own talents.

Keep in mind at all times that money only does two things. It just comes in and goes out. That is all it has ever done and all it ever will do.

My mailbox does not care how many checks come into it each month. I enjoy receiving a pension check, checks from my clients, checks from my broker, and checks from my consulting practice each month. Soon, at age 65, there will be two more pension checks and Social Security. Life is good!

## Recipe for a happy home

When we were married, my aunt and uncle had an artist paint a plate that has hung in every kitchen we have ever had in our forty-three years of marriage. Think of it as baking a life cake:

*To three cups of love and two cups of understanding, add four teaspoons of courtesy and two each of thoughtfulness and helpfulness. Sift together thoroughly, and then stir in an equal amount of work and play. Add three teaspoons of responsibility. Season to taste with study and culture and fold in a generous amount of worship. Place in a pan well greased with security and lined with respect for personality. Sprinkle lightly with a sense of humor. Allow to set in an atmosphere of democratic planning and mutual sharing. Bake in a moderate oven. When well done, remove and top with a thick coating of religious teachings. Serve on a platter of friendliness garnished with smiles.*

My aunt and uncle died many years ago. We got many gifts and presents when we married and all but this one are long gone.

Like your life probably, our lives have been full of joy, sickness, health, heartbreak, successes, and failures.

There are four things that keep our marriage alive and thriving. We are best friends, we love and care deeply for each other, we respect each other, and we meant what we said when we took the marriage vows.

Periodically, we go back to the chapel where we were married and just sit and hold hands and tell stories to each other about the events of our lives and we laugh and giggle. Then, we get up and go back to living and loving as we always have.

She has things she does, I have things I do, and we have things we do. In a nutshell, that is it. The freedom to be loved and respected for who we are as individuals without censorship or complaint is a wonderful thing. No judging. We'll let the big guy do that later when our work here is done.

## Six gifts you must give yourself

When you boil your financial life down to its essence, there are really six gifts you should give yourself. As you read these, read them from the perspective of all the other gifts you have gotten or likely will get in your remaining lifetime. They all are appreciated, but these will insure financial success. You really owe them to yourself; so, why not tie a bow around each one and give yourself the big six.

Give yourself a financial plan based on sound financial principles.

Give yourself a financial plan that is still solid if you become either disabled or die.

Give yourself adequate protection from lawsuits.

Give yourself the gift of a financial plan that minimizes taxes throughout and after your lifetime.

Give yourself the gift of a financial contingency plan in the event of emergencies.

Give yourself a financial blueprint that, when implemented, will provide for a secure and financially independent retirement.

While these gifts on the surface appear to be basic, they are invaluable.

Have you ever let impulse spending or lesser priorities drive your monetary outlays? Have you ever bought things you knew you shouldn't but did it anyway? Each time you do these things robs you of a piece of one of the "big six."

Once you have a comprehensive plan, solid disability and life coverage, protection from lawsuits, tax minimization strategy in place, emergency contingencies covered, and a secure retirement plan, you will be in the best position you have ever been in to be generous.

Give lavishly the gifts of love and time and give financial peace of mind to yourself as a priority. Remember, all the things you either receive or buy during your lifetime can be sold in ninety minutes or less for ten cents on the dollar.

## Why must we own things

Why should I own things that only go down in value and take my time and money to keep them repaired and running properly?

My rationalization for owning clothes boils down to this. Nakedness is not a socially acceptable thing and certainly not so in my case. But, with that said, I own enough clothes to keep me clean, warm and presentable so there will be no more bought by me anytime soon.

Where the point really came to me was when I passed a motor home lot full of expensive moving houses. For $250,000 we could ride in style and see the country. For $2,300 a week, we could do the same thing. We would have a great trip and come home with exactly the same experiences and memories without any of the hassles of ownership. We would simply drive the motor home back onto the lot, remove our belongings, pay our bill and hand them the keys. We will incur no debt. By paying cash for the rental, we will have had no repairs or ownership frustrations and, best of all; we will have invested a reasonable sum in a very good time which we will no doubt remember forever.

The wealthy own a primary home and cars and financial assets. They lease or rent for cash most everything else.

This last summer, we had a family gathering in Frisco, Colorado. A lovely five bedroom place complete with kitchen and fireplace. It was close to everything. Our four children, my brother and his wife and several of our grandchildren were there. We had a wonderful ten days that we all will remember forever. We leased the place, never saw an owner, hit the keypad with the code when we got there, used the place, cleaned it up before we left, paid the bill by mail and left the keys on the kitchen counter.

My purpose in writing this is simply to give you an alternative to ownership. You do not have to own it to use it.

Consider the possibilities and try it just once. My belief is that you will enjoy it and do it over and over again.

## Guess what women fear most

The number one fear for women is the fear of running out of money. The reasons, in my view, that they should be scared are numerous.

Women have yet to achieve anything even close to the same level of earnings as do men. While progress over the last twenty years is noted, they still earn about 24% less and that is the closest to equality of earnings that they have ever had.

If that isn't enough to irritate every woman in America, surely this will. A woman's Social Security check is about two-thirds that of a man's.

Just to pour salt on the already opened wound, let me add that less than one in every five women has a private pension. One of every three men has one.

A woman's annual pension amount is just a little more than 52% of the man's pension.

Retired women have half the annual savings of retired men and it's been that way for a very long time.

Retired women are three times more likely than men to have worked part-time during their working lives.

Women are far more likely to have interrupted their careers to have and raise their children. During this time is when they lost some opportunity to build up their Social Security, pension, and savings.

Finding financial security is different for a woman than for a man. Every woman alive today must understand her own situation and every man must understand his. Couples can blend the data for insight.

As if that isn't enough to make you ill, remember that a woman is likely to live, on average, seven years longer than her man.

Facts are our friends! If these facts do not ignite every woman to get her own purse---nothing ever will.

## Enjoying what we have

One of the words most cherished in our home is *frugality*. The word's definition is "characterized by or reflecting economy in the expenditure of resources." From Latin, *frug* (meaning **virtue**), *frux* (meaning fruit or **value**), and *frui* (meaning to **enjoy** or have use of). So, by my translation, frugality is enjoying the virtue of getting value for every minute of your life and from everything you have the use of. (***Your Money or Your Life***-p.167).

Lives have been transformed in my presence when the meaning of this word *frugal* is understood for the first time.

Frugality means we are to enjoy what we have. One example might be this one. If a woman owns ten dresses but feels she has nothing to wear, she is probably a spender and not a saver or investor. If that same woman owns the same ten dresses and has enjoyed wearing each one of them and still does, she is frugal.

Wastefulness then lies not in the number of possessions you have but in the failure to enjoy each and every one of them. To be successful at being frugal, you must not measure "penny pinching" but instead measure according to the degree of enjoyment you get from the things that come from the material world.

Frugal people get tremendous enjoyment from everything. They sense and appreciate their surroundings. The smell of a rose, a sunset, a child at play, a smile, a hug, a kind word, a roaring fire, a good book, an investment that pays off, some free cash flow, or a new pair of shoes.

What you must develop is a high "joy to stuff" ratio. If you get one measure of joy from each material possession, that's frugal. If you need ten possessions to even begin to register on your "joy meter" you may be missing the whole point of being alive.

If you cannot or do not enjoy the material things you own, could it be that these things symbolize something else to you?

Maybe that something is a sense of "false" worth.

## Your savings could save your financial future

Wouldn't it be nice if we could all be assured of what the future will bring?

Will you really stay with your present employer for the rest of your working life?

Will Social Security really be there for you when it is your turn to retire?

How likely is it in your mind that your present employer will continue to have you pay more and more for the benefits you receive from them?

How comfortable are you with having to depend on your employer and the government providing for your old age?

**One strategy for dealing with these very real issues is to ignore them and that is exactly what the vast majority of working people do today.** That is precisely why they will never end up with sufficient funds to live the life they deserve.

**A better strategy is to do all you can for yourself**. You can develop a mindset that says, "I will save and invest often and wisely and no momentary gratifications will deter me from saving and investing all the money I can and earning all I can on the money I have invested."

Either of these two strategies will get you to that period of your life when you will need income. The question worthy of contemplation is, "Am I more likely to become financially secure depending on my employer and the government, or are my odds improved if I can save and invest over many years wisely?"

My best advice is to maximize what both strategies offer. As soon as you have accumulated your "forget you fund" (six month's living expenses) begin to take advantage of everything your employer offers. Plan using what the government tells you but never trust that they won't change their mind and hurt you in the future. Then, save all you can as fast as you can.

Your contributions plus theirs just might be enough!

## The bank that never closes

As a professional financial planner, you would think the planning of our own financial future with all the puts and takes and calculations and projections would have come naturally; In fact, it did!

With a comprehensive plan in my hand going out to my age ninety-three, my mind began to wander. What if my calculations are not correct? What if something is missing?

With these questions in mind, I scheduled an appointment with another professional planner and hired him to go over every detail of our plan and to give us his personal advice on its strengths and weaknesses.

After his comprehensive review, we sat down together. He praised the depth and thoroughness of the plan. That made me proud! A second opinion that agreed with my own was a good thing. He went on to tell me that in his experience, the fact that my former employer was providing us with medical and dental insurance for life was worth probably in excess of three quarters of a million dollars over our remaining lifetimes. Having never thought of it that way, this input alone was worth the price of the consultation.

Having found no major flaws in my strategic and tactical planning, we relaxed and retired.

In the eight years since retirement it has been proven that the plan was flawed from the start. Neither I nor another planner ever envisioned the impact four children could have on a financial plan. Neither did the plan project that my former employer would start making us pay handsomely for the privilege of having health insurance. That premium alone went up over 600% over the last two years.

When the children have lost jobs, had excessive hospital bills, gotten into debt over their heads, the bank of dad and mom has always been open. When divorce and relocation came up, the bank of dad and mom has always been open.

## In a few words

Abraham Lincoln's Gettysburg address that framed out the character of our nation contained 268 words.

The Declaration of Independence contains 1,300 words.

The Constitution of our nation which has lasted two centuries contains 5,000 words.

The Bible contains 773,000 words.

The federal tax code including its rules and regulations contains 9,000,000 words and grows daily.

Choosing to be a person of few words is a very good thing. It should come as no surprise that the most powerful messages ever delivered have not been lengthy.

It is my view and experience that the trillions of words spoken and written daily concerning what you should do to build your wealth and live happily ever after are nothing more than the bellowing of salespeople. Those messages are primarily produced to get your money out of your pocket and into theirs. Less than one percent of financial knowledge is public knowledge. Most people simply do not realize that what is published is only a very tiny piece of the big puzzle.

The challenge for savers and investors is to tune out virtually all of the "external" messaging being thrown at them daily and to focus on hearing that still quiet voice inside your head that tells you what you want and when you want it.

Making the financial message simple to understand and implement should be the primary goal of truly professional financial planners.

The words that matter are these: **"Spend less than you earn, save a part of every dollar you ever earn, and grow your net worth steadily."** So, in twenty words, you get the big picture. Making these twenty words a part of the life you are living will change your life for the better and make a life of dignity and independence more likely to become a reality for you and your family.

## Whole dollar theory

Many people fail to recognize that most dollars that come into their possession are not whole dollars.

Many people work for wages. They start with a dollar earned, then; the taxes begin. Federal income taxes take a part of the dollar, then we have to pay for Social Security so that takes part of the dollar and then there are Federal Income Contributions act (FICA) deductions and Federal Unemployment Tax Act (FUTA) deductions too. By the way, if you live in a state that has state taxes those will come out of your dollar also. By the time you see the dollar, it has melted to far less than the dollar you earned.

The next type of dollar you get that is a whole dollar at first is a dollar of interest or a dollar in dividends. They look like whole dollars but they are not. At the end of each year, the government says, "Give me my share of those dollars too." Depending on your tax rate, that whole dollar is worth far less than a dollar to you and your family.

When you invest and your investment grows in value it looks like a dollar is a dollar but again it is not. Each year, the government says, "When you sell that investment and pocket a gain, I want a part of those dollars too." So, once a year you settle up and give them a piece of every dollar your investments grew.

Now, when you die, the government says, "Settle up with me within nine months of death and pay me what you owe me in cash before anyone in your family gets a penny if your estate is worth over two million dollars this year."

So, what kind of dollar really is a dollar and stays worth a dollar? Real estate capital gains fit the bill. Be married; accumulate $500,000 or less of capital gains after owning the property for more than two years and each of those dollars stays worth a dollar. The only problem here is you are dependent on the investment growing and in most parts of the country that growth occurs slowly.

It is important to understand the ins and outs of money.

## False expectations appearing real (FEAR)

Ninety-two percent of all the things you fear statistically will never happen. Six percent of the things you fear will happen but they will not be as bad as you expected. Two percent of the things you fear will be worse than your worst nightmare of them.

So, in all my years of supervising, coaching, and teaching, a significant portion of my time has been spent educating people to understand that all but a very small percentage of what they fear will never even happen.

In the business world, employees fear the scorn of a supervisor or anyone in authority who has the "power of the pen." That means the ability to help or harm their business futures. In a proper business environment this fear should not even exist. Great companies offer power, permission, and protection to their people so that their enlightened inputs can become a useful part of constant change.

In academia, the great fear is the fear of failure. Having someone grade your work and tell you whether it meets their standard or not becomes the thing to fear. The fear comes from mental insecurity.

In a personal sense, all the fears of life merge. Being fearful is a choice. You can choose to be afraid or to not be afraid. To face challenges in your life or fear them is a personal choice.

If there is something or anything in your life that you fear, contemplate the source of the fear and then be realistic about the possibility of it ever even occurring.

Personally, you can count me in among those who are afraid of snakes. Knowing that you can either face or avoid fear, my choice is to avoid snakes. Anything else that looks or smells like fear that creeps into my thoughts is faced--- with confidence. Knowing that the odds are in my favor and that a favorable outcome is at the other end of the fear helps me deal with it more effectively.

Dive! Dive! Dive! This is my motto. Take a chance!

## Dealing with the first great loss of my life

All of us have had to deal with great losses in our lives. Let me share with you now the first of mine.

At nineteen, in the only moment of premonition that has ever occurred in my life, somehow, the knowledge came to me that my father was in trouble. He was hospitalized in Dallas with a heart condition and emphysema. I told my boss I did not know why but that I had to leave right then and go to his bedside.

My arrival was within thirty minutes of his death from a massive heart attack. Before the attack, we talked. He knew! He told me to do two things for him. The first was to get my education. The second was to take care of my mother when he was gone. My promise to him was that both would be done. We laughed together, hugged and expressed our love for each other.

Within minutes of that conversation, his breathing labored and nurses and doctors rushed in. They did not even seem to notice me. From the corner where I stood, I watched them slide a board under his back. I watched the doctor literally crawl astride him and beat his fists on his chest. I watched them stick needles into him and work and work and work. Then, suddenly, they stopped. He was gone! At nineteen, he was physically gone from me.

It took me eleven years after that to get my undergraduate degree in night school and five years after that to get my graduate degree. The first of my promises to my father, as I would later learn, was the easy one to keep.

My father is as real to me today as he was that day forty-three years ago. His smile, his laugh, his charm, his temper, his stern instruction, his entrepreneurial insights all are vivid memories. Nothing can or ever will take them from me and for that and for him I am and will always remain eternally grateful.

My mind wanders from time and I wonder what he would have thought of what this son achieved. Then, I smile. He would be one very proud man. I know that for sure!

## Keeping the second promise

Now, a quick fast forward from 1963 when my father died, to September, 2001. An early morning call from the senior center where mother lived set in motion a chain of events no person would ever want to face---a massive stroke with all its implications.

The life flight helicopter arrived about the time I did. Her room was full of firemen and nurses and the pilot. The pilot wanted to put a tube down her throat and had it out. I said, "No!" Running to the butter keeper in her refrigerator, I produced her "Do Not Resuscitate" form. She didn't want that done. The only way I got him to stop was to ask him what he would do if it were his own mother and he knew of the DNR form. He did not use the tube.

All her life, my mother said a person is not what they say nor what they write but they are what they do. For the next eighteen months before her death in March, 2003, she could neither speak nor write.

My mother had fits, tore up her room repeatedly, threw her clothes all over the place and the first time she did that it really made me mad because it embarrassed me. A year later when she tore up her room, I helped her destroy it and it was really fun. Much was learned in that year.

She was in a loving place where her caregivers meant well. They just did not know the strong will of this woman. They were trying to cure her and she was trying to die. When they forced food to her lips in the last weeks of her life, she clamped her lips shut.

This beautiful woman wasted away before my very eyes and going to see her daily and caring for her worldly affairs took me to places in my mind where I had never been before.

By the time mother died, all who loved her knew in their hearts that if she had been a dog or cat, she would have been humanely euthanized at least a year earlier.

My second promise to my father was kept to her dying day.

## Come along with me on this wild ride

First, let's set the stage. Donna and I were both retired by 1997 and we spend every moment we can together. We not only love each other but we are best buds and have been for forty-three years. We travel extensively and most of our travels since retirement have been in one of the five motor homes we have owned.

On this particular evening in October, 2003 (six month after burying mother), we are camped with some of our dearest friends by a lake, watching our campfire burn, wrapped in warm blankets side by side, viewing the most beautiful stars and sky anyone could ever ask to see. It was the start of a magical evening.

Then, in a moment, Donna had a stroke. Before we could even react, her facial muscles fell and her entire right side went numb and became useless. I grabbed her and our friend drove the car. We were twenty minutes from the closest hospital. He drove like a maniac over curbs and down side streets and skidded to a stop in front of the emergency room door. A big, and I mean big, policeman took one look at Donna and scooped her up and ran inside with her in his arms with her arms dangling helplessly at her side. I thought she was going to die right then and right there.

The first thing I was asked since she could not speak was if I had her health care power of attorney. In fact, I did and even had it with me. We carry them in our cars.

It was awful to watch all the stuff they did to her then and later. I shudder to think what might have occurred had someone not been there to speak for her. I knew what she wanted and what she did not want done to her. Our lives are rich and real together but I would have let her go in a heartbeat if they had told me she would have been a vegetable.

Later, she told me she could hear when she could not speak. She heard the words "brain stem injury" and "vegetative" from the nursing staff. Her thoughts were, "Bill, don't let me live like that!" Luckily, I knew that already, because we had prepared for this day.

## The best illness a man could ever have

Without boring you with the details, suffice it to say that I got sick. My last memory was standing in the emergency room telling the nurse of my sickness.

Five days later, awaking from a coma, I hear what I now know was the "death rattle" from the bed next to mine. I couldn't see him because my body had bloated and my eye orbits were swollen shut. I was blind. I hit the buzzer and nurses rushed to my side. "Not me---him," was all I said. He had died of what I had.

My first sight, days later, was my wife in what looked like a bee keeper's hat. I was quarantined.

When they finally figured out what I had (toxic hepatitis) they gave me mega doses of cortisone injected between my toes since those were the only places left that they could find suitable.

All my skin was burned away both inside and outside. I lost all my outer layer of skin. We rolled it down and away like socks and cut the outer layer off with scissors. That took a year to heal.

In the cold still darkness of that hospital room, I prayed this prayer--- "Lord, let me get out of this bed and heal and return to a full and productive life and I promise I will be a better man." He let me live and my life has been lived differently since that moment.

The oldest of our four children was a teenager when this occurred and had it not been for the medical insurance and the disability insurance, I shudder to think what would have become of us all financially during my long period of convalescence.

More importantly, before the illness, I worked sixty to eighty hours a week or more and was the president of the chamber of commerce and held several key civic jobs.

After the illness and the changes made to the way I lived my life, almost every good thing that ever has come my way has occurred.

Being centered on what is important really is important.

## Everybody gets a turn

After seven years of hospice volunteer work and sixty-two years of life, it is clear to me that everyone gets their turn to die.

There is nothing morbid about that statement. It is simply a fact of life. We get born, we live, and then we die.

My God given gifts boil down to just two but both are really good ones. My first gift is the gift of having a strategic, operational and tactical mind that can fairly easily figure things out. My second gift is the ability to work with the elderly and the dying and to get great personal joy and satisfaction from these efforts.

In a practical sense, they are both a blessing and a curse. These two subjects are the two things most people do not want to talk about. They do not want to face the monetary realities of life. Few ever plan their futures, they just move slowly day to day toward it. Even fewer want to face their mortality. Other than in medical or hospice circles, such discussions are almost taboo.

My life's work is to use my skills to educate people to the fact that they can live a dignified and independent life if they will just face the realities of time and money.

Just from what you have read up to now, my father died quickly and relatively inexpensively. My mother died after a long suffering illness that was personally tragic and unbelievably expensive. My wife and I both suffered expensive illnesses that were covered by our insurances. Life and death are both expensive.

What you can and should do to prepare for your inevitable turn is to both get and stay prepared for what may or may not come your way.

Everybody needs to have their financial paperwork in full order at all times. Later, we will go item by item with a listing of all the various things you need to have in place.

Life is a journey---not a destination. Living knowing that you will be dying is a new more meaningful way to think about your existence.

## Meaningful conversations

The most meaningful conversations I have ever held were with those nearing the end of their lives. There is no bravado in those conversations. Nothing is being sold. The comments are from the heart and from the soul. It matters little whether they are financially rich or poor, whether they are young or old, whether they are married or single, whether they are bold or shy. What matters is that they have a few things to say that they really need to say. It is my honor to sometimes be there for those chats.

What strikes me most is that virtually all the people with whom I have ever had a meaningful conversation near the end of their lives really just have three things to say. They say, "Forgive me; I love you, and goodbye." Being there to hear these words spoken in reverence with full meaning even by the feeblest is overpowering in its simplicity.

By translation, what it means to me is the challenge to live a life that will end with no regrets. All the unfinished business will get finished, all those who need to forgive me for something I have done will be asked to forgive me. Those who need to be told they are loved will be told they are loved. When the end is near, a final "goodbye" will be spoken.

Since my personal focus is not on direct care but on the financial debris left for the survivors to clean up, it is important to separate the affairs of the heart and soul from those of the wallet or purse.

If you could only see the messes that are left and the money that is squandered hiring accountants and lawyers and thereby depleting the sums available to heirs, you would drop what you are doing and get your financial affairs in order.

It is my goal to have my final conversation with those I love and who love me be centered on matters of the heart and soul and not on wondering for even one second whether they will be properly cared for in their old age. That paperwork and protective financial shield is now and will stay updated at all times.

## What is included in your estate

Very few people know what the government says makes up your estate for estate tax purposes. Even fewer know how many billions of dollars in estate taxes get collected each year. This money comes from people who, with help, could have avoided paying many of those dollars.

For tax purposes, 50% of the value of any property owned jointly with your spouse (home, automobiles, bank accounts, investments, etc.) must be included.

The full value of any property jointly owned with your children or anyone other than your spouse if they did not contribute to the purchase of the property is in there.

The full value of your Individual Retirement accounts as well as the full value of your 401K, 403B, profit sharing or similar retirement accounts must be included.

The full value of your life insurance death benefits must also be counted.

How about this one? The value of your pension survivorship element (example: your spouse gets 50% of your monthly pension after your death).

Lastly, the full value of any property owned in your own name.

Proposed changes get introduced every year and you can bet they won't be designed to save you or your heirs any money.

Our government has a wolf like appetite for our dollars and they seldom miss a chance to eat from our money bucket.

As if all this isn't enough, my favorite thing is that if your estate is big enough (2M in 2006) they demand to get paid in cash within nine months of your death. A pretty cold approach when you consider that many estates of that size come from individual business owners and owners of farms and ranches that will have to be sold at fire sale prices to get the cash needed to just pay the estate taxes within the stated timeframe.

They tax every dollar over and over again! It never ends!

## Protect your greatest assets

Protecting assets is a little discussed area. The reason it so seldom is discussed is because the financial press is always trying to "advantage themselves with your money."

What we must do is "advantage you." The advantage must always put the odds in your favor to the greatest extent possible.

First, get an education and keep your skills modern. Think of yourself as a business. Your employer hired you on potential but will keep you based on the skills you bring to the next assignment. Your power to earn is your greatest asset. Education gives you an advantage.

Next, let's talk about your health. Get regular checkups, workout, walk, meditate, and invest in yourself and your well being. Without health, you have nothing. Without health you cannot work nor earn. Maintaining good health advantages you.

Insure against all risks that disadvantage you. The chances of being disabled are five times more likely than dying. So, why do so many people have life insurance and so few have comprehensive disability insurance? By protecting your earning power, you gain a financial advantage.

Insure your life with term insurance. They bet you live and you get the protection. If you die, your heirs get paid. Protecting your lifestyle for those you love is a duty. The advantage goes from you to your loved ones.

All you have to have is one disability or one long extended stay in a hospital to fully understand how cheap health and disability insurance premiums truly are.

The common thread in all these items is that the asset you are protecting is you. Protecting against financial devastation brought your way by surprise or circumstances beyond your control.

When told by clients that they cannot afford to protect their assets, my reply is always the same. "You really cannot afford not to!"

You must anticipate and prepare for your uncertain future.

## Genius thinking

A smart person learns from their own mistakes and a genius learns from the mistakes of others.

After years of working with men and women of all ages and circumstances, several patterns of behavior merge in my mind and simply get repeated over and over by other people. They never seem to change.

People seem to want instant gratifications. They want what they want and they want it right now. Such a mentality naturally gravitates to debt. Since they do not have the money to pay for the things they want right now, they simply borrow and borrow and borrow some more. Before long, they never really think of saving and investing, they just want to see if they can squeeze the monthly payment into their lives. Such thinking has ruined and continues to ruin millions of lives.

Most simply exist from day to day. They have no plans or documented dreams. They never calculate what they own nor owe and they have no clue about their net worth. They never contemplate retiring because they think they can't and so they spend what they earn and borrow beyond that to make themselves feel momentarily good.

The lack of monetary discipline stands out to me. Being neither willing nor able to save or invest monthly is a clear sign of lack of discipline. Those who cannot save simply are being unrealistic about what their aging and physical health will cost them.

Most never calculate nor manage their tax burdens. They accept them as if there is nothing they can do to manage some of the costs down. Delaying the payment of taxes while your savings and investments grow tax deferred is a very powerful wealth building strategy that is under used by most working people.

Lastly, most fail to insure themselves against the catastrophic expenses that just might happen to them.

Be aware of these pitfalls and manage them all away.

## A lesson taught to me in the back yard

For more than twenty-five years, a Spanish couple and their family mowed our yard, raked our leaves, cared for our shrubbery and did all those tasks that needed to be done. They are a wonderful family and we consider them to be a part of ours.

Just before the death of my mother when she was wasting away right before my very eyes, while working in the back yard, Olivia was trimming one of our hedges. As I watered the flower bed beside her, she looked over to me with the hedge trimmer humming and said, "How is your mom doing?" Truly, I was momentarily speechless.

I must have waited just a little too long. Olivia turned off the hedge trimmer, looked me straight in the eye and said, "Don't worry Mr. Knight, she has a good soul and she will be fine."

She did have a good soul and she in fact soon would be fine. What that wonderful woman taught me that afternoon was how sweet it would be to say to anybody who loves someone who was nearing death that that person they loved had a good soul and would be fine.

Just over a year ago, Olivia's husband, Fidel, suffered a paralyzing stroke and his rehabilitation has been slow. They were building a new home away from our hometown and after all those years of helping us, they moved out of state.

Just recently, as I pondered the question, "Wonder what ever happened to Fidel?" Immediately, my next thought was the one Olivia shared with me that day in the back yard. There is no need to worry about either Olivia or Fidel, they each have a good soul and they will be fine.

I know what love is and through my volunteer work with hospice, periodically, I really reach all the way inside my soul.

Whatever the future holds, it is all a part of the experience of living. It is my intention to live a life without regrets. A life filled with personal peace, financial security, and genuine happiness is my quest. I really want a good soul.

## When somebody dies somebody cleans up

One day not long ago, the hospice office called and asked if we would go help a new widow sort out some of the paperwork she had that pertained to the medical bills she and her husband had accumulated during his eighteen month losing battle with brain cancer. We agreed and called this lovely woman and went to her home.

Upon arrival, she invited us in and took us through the closed door that led to her dining room. On that table, heaped in a huge mound, were literally hundreds of opened and un-opened medical bills. From end to end, this table that seated eight was at least a foot high in the middle with nothing but bills.

When Donna and I saw it, we looked at each other and grinned. We knew this supposedly simple request had suddenly become on heck of a big and nasty job.

Without another word, we assisted this grieving woman as we started on the north corner and worked our way to the south end of the table. Thank goodness we got there early in the day. By sunset, we had all the stuff sorted by hospital, doctor, pharmacy, and insurance company.

We had identified a full page list of issues that had to be resolved. Situations where the primary insurance had not been handled first or where the secondary had not been contacted at all or where a partial and inaccurate payment had been made to one or the other. The errors were numerous and each impacted the financial life of this wonderful woman.

After several weeks of work, the list was down to one item. It was my personal favorite. The husband was taken by life flight helicopter to a distant city where he had brain surgery the next day. The surgery revealed the inoperable brain tumor. They closed his head back up. Two days later, an ambulance took him back to one of our local hospitals. The life flight helicopter bill was paid in full but both the primary and secondary insurers rejected the payment of his ambulance ride home. We had to pay that bill.

## Selfish loved ones

The things people do for money never ceases to amaze me. The things people do to people they supposedly love amazes me even more.

Here is one of those stories. A man we will call K has been married to his second wife for twelve years. He is diagnosed with a fatal disease and realizes that he has not updated his will to make sure his wife is taken care of when he dies. He asks one of his daughters to get the will done for him and they go to a meeting with her lawyer and the work begins.

Days, weeks, and months go by and no will appears. Naturally, K becomes concerned because he realizes his health is deteriorating quickly and he cannot be certain he will live long enough to get this new will completed. Contacts with both the daughter and the lawyer by the second wife produce no results.

With only a few days of life left, it was learned that the daughter does not like the second wife, does not want her to have any of her father's money and wants the full estate to go to her side of the family. It was she who was intentionally dragging out the paperwork in direct opposition to the stated desire of her father.

Putting ourselves in harms way, we became convinced that we understood what was going on but rather than get into legal jeopardy, we got another lawyer to go the bedside of this dying man and get his last will done in world record time.

Within days of completing this work, K died. He died with the will completed and with a second wife who literally would have been financially devastated had this work not gotten completed.

In hospice work, we learn that all our efforts are devoted to taking care of the physical, spiritual, and practical needs of those we serve. It is all about them and them alone.

Money brings out the worst in people. That daughter is probably still out there in an angry mood because, in the end, she did not get her way.

## Permanent income theory

When you think of income, what is your frame of reference? Most people consider the wages they earn from their employer as permanent income. Such income is in fact temporary. Lose the job and you lose the income stream.

When your point of reference becomes the generation of permanent income, your whole approach to money immediately shifts. So, you ask, "What is permanent income?"

Permanent income is an income stream that is dependable, reliable, and which will last forever whether you are employed or not. More specifically, it is the income your savings, investments and assets will generate for the remainder of your lifetime.

Your goal should be to save and invest as much as you can as often as you can and to keep up with the amount of income your savings, investments, and assets will generate for you forever.

An easy way to calculate the percentage of your lifestyle expenses your savings, investments, and assets will provide is to take today's thirty year treasury bond rate (currently 4.43%) and multiply that rate times the total of all your savings and investments.

If monthly outflows are $4,000 and the total of all your investments is $50,000. At 4.43%, you have permanent income of $2,215 a year. That number divided by 12 (months) gives you permanent monthly income of $184.58.

Your permanent income percentage is 4.6%. Yes! That is the correct number. Fifty thousand dollars of free and clear wealth, in this present low interest rate environment generates paltry sums of permanent income.

Even a millionaire's permanent annual income would only be $44,300 before tax or $3,691.67 a month. This sum would hardly be enough to live a life of luxury in old age.

Working towards building up your investment balances and building your permanent income percentage to 100% is the goal.

## Why we all do not end up millionaires

A few years ago, I attended a financial seminar where the speaker made becoming rich sound so easy. Just earn $30,000 a year. Save 10% of your salary and have your employer match 50% of the first 6% a year and have the investments earn 6%. As if by magic, this 25 year old at age 65 would have $803,750. By earning 10% on the investments for those 40 years, he/she would have $2,582,341. At 8% the sum would be $1,416,295. Doesn't that all sound easy?

So, why isn't everybody by age 65 a millionaire? Having become fascinated with this question over the years and after spending thousands of hours figuring out why the exact opposite becomes true for ninety-nine of every hundred people, some of my findings are worth contemplation.

Finding a job at age 25 that pays $30,000 is not all that easy. For those without education, it is actually quite difficult.

Saving 10% of a $30,000 salary is something that few have the discipline to do every month of their working lives.

Many employers do not, will not, and never have matched 50% of the first 6% employees save in their savings plan retirement accounts.

Earning 6% per year much less 8% or 10% requires investment. Imagine trying to project yourself into the future right now and say, "I know how to earn 10% on my investments each year for the next 40 years." It just is not that easy.

Not many live beneath their means so they have no savings. What they do have is the great destroyer of wealth---debt. So, they never get ahead, never save, never have free cash flow, and never invest to secure their financial futures.

Few realize that money needs time to grow. So--- save, save, and save some more.

Money gets sucked away first by taxes, then by debt, then by excessive expenses. Poof! Your financial future is gone forever.

## Life is an expensive adventure

If you want to really scare yourself silly, think about some of these things.

How much interest will you pay out over your lifetime on a home?

How much money will you pay out on credit card interest and other consumer forms of debt?

How much money will you pay out to raise and educate your children?

How much money will you pay out to buy perishable goods (things that wear out or get used up)?

How much interest over your lifetime will you pay out on automobile debt?

How badly will you need much of that money you have paid out over the years to generate permanent income for you when you retire?

How much money will you have paid out in all forms of taxation since you got your first job?

How badly has inflation impacted your purchasing power over the years?

How much money have you earned during your lifetime and how much of it do you have in total right now?

How good is your health and how much is it likely to cost you over the rest of your life?

The point being made here is that you will be and are constantly barraged with things that demand an outflow of your funds. They are always present and tend to creep up on you.

**Money just comes in and goes out and that is all it ever has done or ever will do**. Learning how to consciously maximize the inflows and rigorously control the outflows is one big secret to financial success.

While doing consulting work for a billionaire, I asked him what it was like to be worth a billion dollars. His reply was that it costs a lot of money to be a billionaire. *His focus was on the cost*!

## The flicker of the flame

As a part of my hospice work, from time to time, my role is to speak to a gathered group of men and women who meet monthly at a bereavement luncheon sponsored by the hospice.

Anyone who has lost a loved one is invited to attend and each meeting features a speaker. My topic is always how to deal with the paperwork that has to be dealt with before, during, and after the death of a loved one.

Each time I attend one of these luncheons, I am struck by all that goes into having one. The meals are always paid for by a sponsoring business or individual. The decorations are always done by two sisters who use their creative gifts in this special way. The attendees are always a mixture of the young, middle aged, and elderly. Men and women mix together in an atmosphere of reverent sharing. All have shared the same experience.

Some have attended these monthly luncheons for years. Others just come once in a while. By observing carefully, one learns that people grieve and mourn in their own ways and on their own timetables and that it is perfectly appropriate to grieve and mourn any way one chooses for as long as necessary.

At this particular luncheon, the bereavement coordinator had us all do a special exercise. She gave us a candle and had us light it. She asked us to think of that candle as the life of the person we loved who had been lost. She asked us to focus on the flame and to watch the candle burn down. We were to isolate our minds on nothing but that candle and that flame.

Imagine this room with thirty-three candles burning. Then, she asked that we let them go. She asked us when we were ready to put out the candle. To enjoy it for as long as we liked but to try to put it out if we could.

I participated that day because I was the guest speaker. What I actually ended up doing was releasing the grief I had stored inside my soul. I put out the first candle and then a second. I, that day, in that special place, let my father and mother go.

## Plotting financial independence

Financial independence can be plotted on a simple graph. All you have to know is the plot points.

First, we would have to plot our incoming money (cash in/revenues) from all sources for any month, any year, or any decade. To do this plotting, just get out a sheet of paper and use the vertical axis for money and the horizontal axis for time. Then, simply start plotting.

Right about here is where almost all people fall off the wagon. They fail to understand that when you leave the "for pay" period of your life, money coming from work ceases to exist. It is gone! So, that money must be replaced with cash earned from your savings, investment, and retirement account balances.

Next, we have to plot the cash going out. The amount of money you spend. This figure is an actual and it includes all your fixed and variable expenses. They are what they are until you learn how to manage them down or up depending on your personal preferences. The key question here is, "What can you afford to spend?"

The third plot point is the dollar inflows that will come from your savings, investment, and retirement accounts without depleting even a penny of the principal. Use the safe 30 year Treasury bond yield for this calculation.

You will not be financially independent until your third plot point intersects with your expense plot point. When it does, you are indeed, at that moment, financially independent.

You will learn in retirement that the control of outflows is easier than is the stimulation of inflows.

What we are seeking is the ideal state of "enough." Enough to live comfortably, enough to do the things we do now, and enough to last us the rest of our lives barring catastrophe which we protect against with insurances.

By planning and plotting you will know when you can expect to be financially independent.

## The perfect day

From podiums across America, from coast to coast, on numerous occasions over the years, I've demonstrated to individuals and groups how life gets squandered.

From each audience, I get three volunteers to come join me on stage. Each is asked to describe to me what would be a "perfect day" from the moment they wake up until the moment they go to sleep. Over the years, some truly interesting tales have been told.

What I'd like you, the reader, to do is simply sit quietly for a few moments and ponder the question yourself. Then, answer it for yourself. No two answers have ever been the same.

Your life is unique! You get to make all the choices! The things you do each day should bring you joy, personal peace, inner harmony, love and true happiness. Removing from your life those things that do not provide these nourishments to your soul is noble work.

What would it be worth to be able to spend every waking moment with those you love doing only the things that bring you joy and happiness?

Trudging off to a job that provides only a paycheck and takes you away from all that truly matters in life makes little sense when you consider that an alternative is available.

Realizing that you can have virtually anything you want in life, just not everything, is a key component of finding and fulfilling your life's purpose.

Every day should be opened like the precious gift that it truly is.

At the end of every session where people have been asked to describe their perfect day, each has done so with a joyous smile on their face. They literally love to do this exercise.

It always ends the same way. Each is asked, "When did you last have a perfect day?" The answer from them is always the same, "I never have!"

Maybe tomorrow should be your perfect day!

## Up and down the slippery slope

There is a slippery slope each of us must pay attention to as we move through life. That slippery slope goes up one side and down the other. The upside of the slope is the impact inflation will have on your retirement income. Retire today with $1,000 a month income. With 5% inflation, after five years, you will need $1,276 to buy what $1,000 buys today. Twenty five years from today you will need $3,386 to buy what $1,000 buys today. So, that is the nasty upslope.

The nasty down slope shows the impact that same 5% inflation will have, over time, on the future purchasing power of the $1,000 in today's dollars. After five years, the $1,000 will purchase you goods and services valued at $774. At twenty five years, your $1,000 has eroded to the point it will only buy $277 in today's money.

So, there you have it. Inflation has a dramatic impact on both your income and purchasing power through time.

Every calculation you make about your future must include assumptions about inflation. Even then, they may be wrong and probably will be. The only way to be safe is to be extremely conservative with your projections.

Inflation does not matter to you if you are not buying goods and services that have inflated. If you keep the old car and do not buy the new one that costs 20% more, you have dodged its inflation.

If you own your home free and clear, inflation works for you by driving up the value of your property.

When inflation drives up interest rates, it is good for the saver. More money is earned on the money you have saved.

Some things inflate far faster than do other things. Health care and health care premiums inflate much faster than overall inflation and you must properly estimate those costs as you age.

Inflation is always present and it is extremely harmful to those who have not properly prepared for its impacts.

## Walk a mile in these shoes

FM was a wonderful woman I had known all my life because she was the sister of one of my oldest friends.

She carried an oxygen tank everywhere she went because her long years of smoking had charred her lungs.

One night, feeling ill, her husband R called 911. She was taken to the hospital immediately and from there she underwent numerous procedures she later told me she never would have wanted done had she been able to tell the doctors and nurses her wishes. She had no durable health care power of attorney and nobody could speak for her---not even her husband.

After heroic procedures, FM lived and went to a nursing home.

Her brother called me and asked if I'd come to her bedside and get her to sign the health care power of attorney since she had refused to do so. I went! At her bedside, I told her the story of my mother and how useful it had been to have this paperwork in order. She signed the documents and I got a stranger in the hallway to sign as a witness since nobody that worked at the nursing home was allowed to witness the document (afraid of being sued).

FM eventually got better, went home and lived another eight months.

During her final hospital stay, FM initially did not want her brother to execute the health care power of attorney. When the nurses would leave the room, she would remove her oxygen mask and smoke a cigarette (she was truly addicted). She still thought she might live.

On the last day she could speak, she asked that the powers of attorney be invoked and from that moment forward her brother spoke for her.

She spent her last day gasping from one breath to the next but she did it by personal choice. It was what she wanted. She had had enough and nobody was to try to cure her any longer.

## A grandchild inherits wealth

First, a grandfather dies without a will. Then, the grandmother gets a will of her own but dies before the final clean up is complete from the debris left when her husband died without a will. They owned property all over the country and even some in Mexico. They had sold their dry cleaning businesses years before and had traveled extensively. They were supported by a broker who had them in investments far too risky for people of their ages and an accountant and tax man who were less than fully competent.

The grandmother leaves it all to her granddaughter. She calls me and we begin the work of first finding everything, probating the grandmother's will and then identifying all the issues that would need to be addressed before the money could be distributed properly to her.

Lawyers had to be hired in several states and probating the will and getting letters testamentary was a hassle.

Two years later, everything had been found and a new tax man had been hired, the broker had been fired, and a new account had been set up at a discount brokerage.

The wealth was substantial for a young woman with a young family. She was an inexperienced saver and investor.

We prepared her dream list. It included a brand new home, new furnishings, and a new truck for her husband. Also, it included a wish to have no debt whatsoever.

With her dream list completed, she went about the business of fulfilling her dreams. She bought the house and the truck and furnished the house beautifully. All her debts were paid in full.

When it was revealed to her that she never had to take one penny's risk in the stock market and that she could retire early with an estimated net worth in excess of six million dollars, she was first floored and then elated.

A broker would have told her to go for fifteen million. Why?

## The day I got mad at God

Getting mad at God is not a good thing to do but I sure did it not long ago.

It was one of those days when I was having a "pity party" of my own and the weight of seeing all the pain and suffering people went through as they neared death just hit me right between the eyes. I got really mad and prayed, "Why are you doing this to these people?" I got no reply!

My mind focused on the cumulative effect this hospice work was having on my mind. The people with whom I worked were plain ordinary people just trying to live useful and productive lives. Then, wham! They can't work, they get sicker, they lose their dignity and independence because they run out of money and they live their last days in emotional agony. I prayed again, "This is just not right---stop it!" Again, I got no reply.

By now, I had really worked myself into an emotional fit. Could it be that my thinking was not right?

I went outside the nursing home and sat on a bench and watched the clouds roll by. I thought and thought. Then, just as suddenly as my anger had come, it was gone. Something new and wonderful came to me.

God wasn't doing all these bad things to these folks; it was just part of the experience of life. He was there to give me the strength to endure whatever might come my way. He was there to give each of them that strength that passes human understanding. This time I prayed, "God, am I right? Are you there to give me strength in time of need?" He did not answer me but just as I said that prayer, one of the most beautiful clouds I've ever seen moved over head and somehow I knew---I just knew I was onto something wonderful.

I'm never going to get mad at God again and if I had been a better student, I would not have gotten mad the first time.

It is the experience of living that holds meaning for us all.

## Goofy things

The human mind really can make people do peculiar things. Some are cute, some are sad, and most are expensive.

Once upon a time there was a wealthy client who simply piled up his brokerage statements on the corner of his desk for a year because he did not want to confront what they said. He knew down deep what they said, but he did not want to see it in reality. It was too painful. That wealthy client is far wealthier today than he was that day and the only major difference is that we got the risk out of his portfolio and created goals and timelines for meeting those goals that have proven to be both proper and realistic.

Once upon a time there was the man who created a trust to make sure his daughter could not get all his money at once. It was to be paid to her by the trustee at $1,000 per month. The only thing he forgot was to put his certificates of deposit into the trust. Had we not caught that error, his daughter would have gotten almost $200,000 in cash by simply presenting his death certificate to the credit union. This was not at all what he wanted; he just did not pay attention to details. We fixed that in one visit.

How about the client who hired me to help her get out of debt? She had plenty of it and we worked diligently for ten months to reduce it substantially. Then, one night about 11pm the phone rings and she wakes me up. She says, "Haven't I been doing good reducing my debts?" My grogged response was, "Yes you have." "Good," she said, "I just bought myself a fifteen thousand dollar ring my husband doesn't know anything about and I'm so happy." I fired her on the spot and went back to sleep.

My personal favorite is this one. An executive hired me to do a complete financial plan for him. He paid me up front in full and went home to fill out the initial paperwork. After six monthly follow ups, he had sent me nothing. After a year, I offered to refund his money since I had done not one thing for him. He would not hear of it. He said, "I want to remember how dumb I can be!"

## A grand man losing it all

Ever have a dear friend that just breaks your heart! Such a friend was H. We became friends years ago and we watched him make and lose two fortunes. He was an opportunist and a genuine risk taker. In the 1980's, he built luxury homes on speculation that someone would buy them all. The bottom dropped out of the market and he lost everything. Another great adventure for him was oil and gas with all its ups and downs. He went up and then he went down.

After losing his second fortune, he took a great job and held it until retirement but he never regained his financial strength. Somewhere along the way, he became bitter. He knew what he had had and he knew full well what he had lost.

On our next to last visit together, his wife was losing both her mind and her eyesight. His only real outlet had become an occasional round of golf. He was confined to his home to care for his ailing wife.

On our last visit together, he had sold his home and moved into a small apartment. His lovely wife did not even recognize him anymore and her nursing home costs were soaking up his modest means quickly. He was preparing to move back to his hometown and take her there too where costs were more modest.

This was a man who had it all twice. Not once! Twice! He never anticipated losing everything and he never prepared properly for an uncertain future.

He became so crotchety and grumpy that it was almost impossible to be with him even when we really wanted to.

His is a story of a life full of wonderful memories now spoiled by having to face old age and infirmity without adequate funding.

He has lost his dignity and his independence and along with that he lost his way. The end of his life will not be what we anticipated and for me and mine that is really sad.

I really miss the old H. He was a heck of a guy in his prime.

## Mr. Lucky

One of my distant relatives is the luckiest man alive. His story is a remarkable tale told only to show how enough money coming in can overpower a tub load of spending sin.

Ever since I've known him he has been in debt up to his ears. He is now in his eighth decade of life and he still is in debt up to his ears.

He has been known to have in his closet box after box of expensive shoes he has never even worn. Shirts he has never had on and suits that still have the tags on them.

He has had big homes with big debts. Big expensive cars—always! He has had the beach homes and all the toys a man could ever ask for.

He has lived a life of luxury from the get go. By now, you must be asking how he was able to do all that. It was easy! He held a big job at a big company for over forty years. The company had a generous menu of benefits and an even more generous retirement plan. His big corporate title gave him access to money. Bankers showered him with credit. All he had to do was ask.

He is the exact opposite of what I teach and preach. Yet, it has worked for him.

The corporate America he worked in is for the most part gone. The days of defined benefit pensions, free healthcare, generous annuities and deferred compensation schemes is becoming obsolete.

Had he been a young man now entering the workforce instead of a senior citizen who took full advantage of every benefit his company offered, he would be in a world of hurt forty years from now.

The risks of building future wealth now mostly fall on the shoulders of the worker not on the backs of the employer. The risks have shifted.

The luckiest man I know would be a truly unlucky man indeed had he entered the workforce last year.

## Important ratios for individuals

Every one of us is a business. You should operate your business using some important calculations that are easy to do.

Over the last twelve months, how much has your net worth grown (all you own minus all you owe)?" Take that number and divide it by your net worth one year ago. That number is your net worth percentage return. You will need for this figure to be 15% per year before retirement in order to insure financial independence. The earlier you start calculating, the better chance you have.

Another simple yet powerful calculation is daily cash flow. Figure out your total income per day and divide that number by your total expenses per day. The result must be greater than 1.00 or you are losing ground. When you get this number to 2.00 you will know you have substantial free cash flow to save and invest. Achieving this 2.0 result is critical to your financial future.

Quick coverage is another of my favorites. Just add up all the immediately available cash you have (every dollar) and divide that number by your average monthly expenses minus all taxes. This will let you see how vulnerable you are to the unexpected. Since you want to first have what I call "forget you funds" that equal six months of your average monthly expenses salted away safely at all times, you will need this ratio to produce a result of at least 6.00. Below that and you are taking risks. What if you lost your job, got hurt?

The last is personal leverage. This one gets at your solvency. Get a total of all your liquid assets (cash you could get your hands on in thirty days) and divide that number by the value of your total debts. Unless that number is 1.00 or higher, you are giving the economic advantages of time and compound interest to someone else (your lenders). With a result above 1.0, you begin to have the monetary advantage.

During our wealth building years, we used all these regularly. You may find them valuable too. I truly hope so.

## What is the purpose of work

Many years ago, Joe Dominguez and Vicki Robin really taught me something important. Let me share some thoughts from their book, ***Your Money or Your Life (pp 228-229)***.

This is my own version of what I took from their thoughts and ideas on the topic of work.

Some people work to earn money so they can provide necessities, comforts, and luxuries and to provide funds for the causes they champion. Others, just to have it and to leave an estate.

For others, it simply gives a sense of security. It is a measure of your worth and how you keep score.

Tradition comes into play for those who follow a parent into a particular profession or business. There is a continuity that is viewed as both important and essential.

Then there is duty. Doing what you are supposed to do so that society will function smoothly.

Some work to serve others. To make what for them is a better town or state or country or world.

Still others work to learn new skills that they can exploit for gain.

Power is an aphrodisiac. It insists that people follow your commands or gives you significant influence over what others must do.

Just being with others is reason enough to work for some in the workplace.

Lastly, people work for personal growth and intellectual stimulation. Their goal is to be challenged or to expand their emotional or intellectual lives.

My purpose in paraphrasing their words is to have you pause and take a few minutes to explore the question.

As it turns out, after retirement, it is easier to see why I worked. It was a means to an end. They used me and I used them. They had things they wanted from me and I had things I wanted from them. They got what they wanted and I did too. It worked!

## Cassandra

As a student of Greek and especially Latin, stories from Greek mythology have always interested me.

As my work as a financial planner, wealth builder, and hospice volunteer progressed over the last decade and a half, there is one story from Greek writings that has true meaning in my work.

Cassandra was the daughter of King Priam and Queen Hecuba of Troy. Apollo was smitten by this beautiful child. He let her sleep in his temple among his pet snakes. They licked her ears and passed on to her the secrets of prophecy.

Apollo watched her grow up and fell in love with her. She stayed in the temple again and gave him just one kiss. He wanted more. Apollo was so disappointed when the kiss did not last long enough for him that he dribbled a bit and the power of belief was washed away from her.

From that moment forward, whatever she predicted (which was always true), was never believed by anyone who heard her words. She was described as being "mad as a hatter."

Nearing the end, Cassandra knew she would be raped, given away and finally murdered by Clytemnestra. Nobody believed her but all her prophesies became truth.

My reason for sharing this story with you is because I feel like Cassandra.

With part of the proceeds from my mother's estate I opened an office where all people had to do was come and ask for help. Most of the practice was free to all comers. I closed that office a few months ago---never to open it or any other again.

The pain of seeing people come to me, get my help, and in some cases pay me big bucks and then to watch them go away and do absolutely nothing to help themselves was more than I could stand.

The financial future of millions is clear to me but not to them. They cannot see what I can see. Cassandra knows and so do I. Not complaining, life is good for me--just explaining and sharing.

## The big close

For those of you who know what you need to do but just haven't gotten around to doing it yet, consider this my best effort to get you moving.

You are getting older every single day. A day where you have saved nothing at all is a day of poverty you have built for yourself at the end of life.

Time and money wait for no one! If you have wasted this day then shame on you. If you have spent his day doing anything you did not want to do then re-think tomorrow.

Life is so incredibly short and my choice is to never waste another breath "suffering for the foolish."

On the next three pages you will find a document checklist that took me years and years to thoroughly research and compile. If you will take it and use it, you will have done a wonderful thing for those who must clean up behind your financial elephant.

While we all came into this world with nothing, we will leave it with "stuff and things" that have to be disposed of properly and in accordance with rules, regulations and laws. No choice! They have to be dealt with and we all have to meet our maker and pay the piper.

What a gift it will be to leave our worn out bodies and enjoy eternity with our maker free of pain and suffering.

What a gift it will also be to leave your worldly affairs in perfect order so that nobody else has to clean up behind you. Why should anyone else have to clean up your mess?

There are enough ideas and tactics included inside this book for any reasonable person to apply to their personal situations.

Of several things I am convinced. If you do not want to live the last years of your life as a ward of the state or federal government, you better hurry up and start saving and facing the realities of life.

There! I feel better now. May you all find your own personal peace, health, happiness and financial independence!

## The key document checklist

| The Document | Yes/No | Notes |
|---|---|---|
| 1. Durable Power of Attorney | | |
| 2. Durable Health Care Power of Attorney | | |
| 3. Living Will | | |
| 4. Do Not Resuscitate form | | |
| 5. Will | | |
| 6. Trust Documents | | |
| 7. Medicare Card | | |
| 8. Supplemental Insurance Card | | |
| 9. Property Deeds | | |
| 10. Auto titles | | |
| 11. Brokerage Account Numbers and access instructions | | |
| 12. Brokerage Accounts latest year-end statements | | |
| 13. Last year's tax return | | |
| 14. Doctor's name and telephone number | | |
| 15. Lawyer's name and telephone number | | |

| | | |
|---|---|---|
| 16. CPA's name and telephone number | | |
| 17. Financial and estate oversight advisor's name and telephone number | | |
| 18. Estate attorney's name and telephone number | | |
| 19. Social Security cards | | |
| 20. Marriage License | | |
| 21. Safe/lock box combinations & keys | | |
| 22. General letter of instruction for use in handling estate/probate | | |
| 23. Checking Acct. Information | | |
| 24. Beneficiary Verifications | | |
| 25. Life Insurance Policy Information | | |
| 26. Military Discharge Papers | | |
| 27. Birth Certificates | | |
| 28. Loan Information | | |
| 29. Credit Card Information | | |

| | | |
|---|---|---|
| 30. Charitable Donation Information and wishes | | |
| 31. Certificate of Deposit Information | | |
| 32. Treasury Direct Information | | |
| 33. Savings Account Information | | |
| 34. Right of Survivorship agreement-if married | | |
| 35. Long-term care policies | | |
| 36. Disability policies | | |
| 37. All information in one place and someone in the family is aware of where that place is. | | |

Who speaks for you when you cannot speak for yourself?
Where is all your financial paperwork?
Who knows where your money is kept?
How much money will your estate spend that could have been avoided?
Who knows your last wishes?
What do you want done to you when you are hospitalized?
How easy will it be for your heirs to access your money?

These are but some of the questions that get answered when your financial paperwork is in order. This, in my view, is the duty you have to those you love and who love you.

It is expensive, time consuming, and heartbreaking to expect loved ones during an emotional crisis to dig through your desk, home, and mailbox trying to find clues to what you have and where you have it.

Those who find, organize, and keep current their financial affairs are more likely to distribute more of their wealth to the people and causes they champion.

This list is comprehensive and includes everything I've ever seen used to move trust and probate funds to heirs efficiently.

Make it a point to not only gather this data but to also go over it with someone who will be administering it after you are gone.

Should you need professional help understanding any of the issues or ideas expressed in this book, contact me electronically at bknight51@charter.net. I will personally respond to any thought, idea or question you have so long as you commit that you will use the thoughts and ideas to better your financial future.

Barring tragedy, my financial future is secure. It is yours that now interests me.

Not long ago, a business associate asked me why I seemed to be so focused on people when they are at their very worst. My response was both immediate and heart felt. "It is when they are the most interesting and when they listen best."

My intention is to live fully from here, knowing that my turn is coming. That fateful day when my earthly life is over will be here soon enough. It is my choice to not surround myself with those who berate my best efforts or undermine my dreams. They have no right to my days anymore than I have a right to theirs.

Free choice and free will are meaningful words to me. I will love those who love me and be with those I can truly help!

You can order this book from www.lulu.com, from my web site, www.moneydr.com, or you can ask your favorite bookstore to order it for you.

www.ingramcontent.com/pod-product-compliance
Lightning Source LLC
Chambersburg PA
CBHW081214170526
45165CB00009B/2819